A postcard for you
to color and mail.

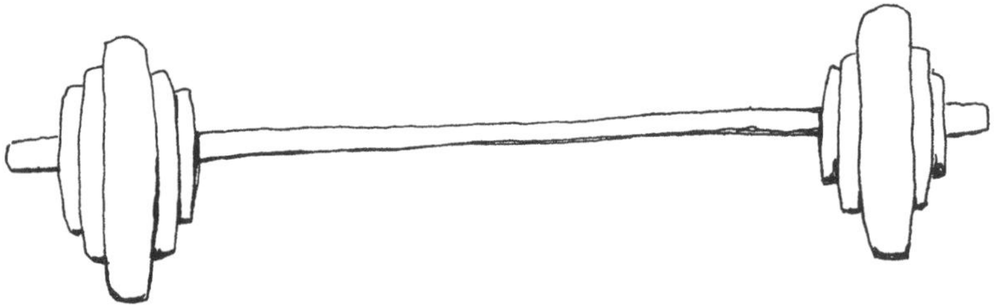

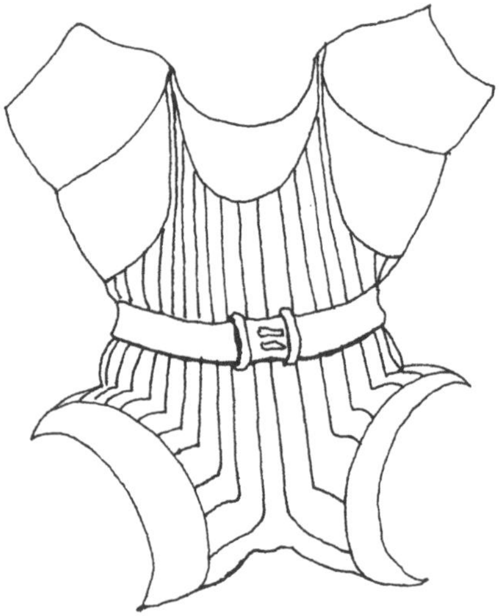
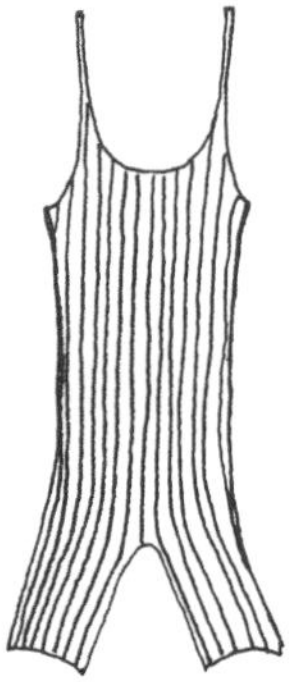

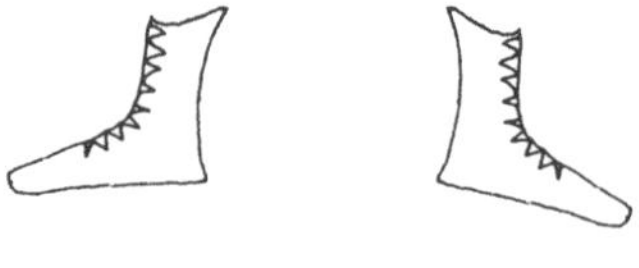

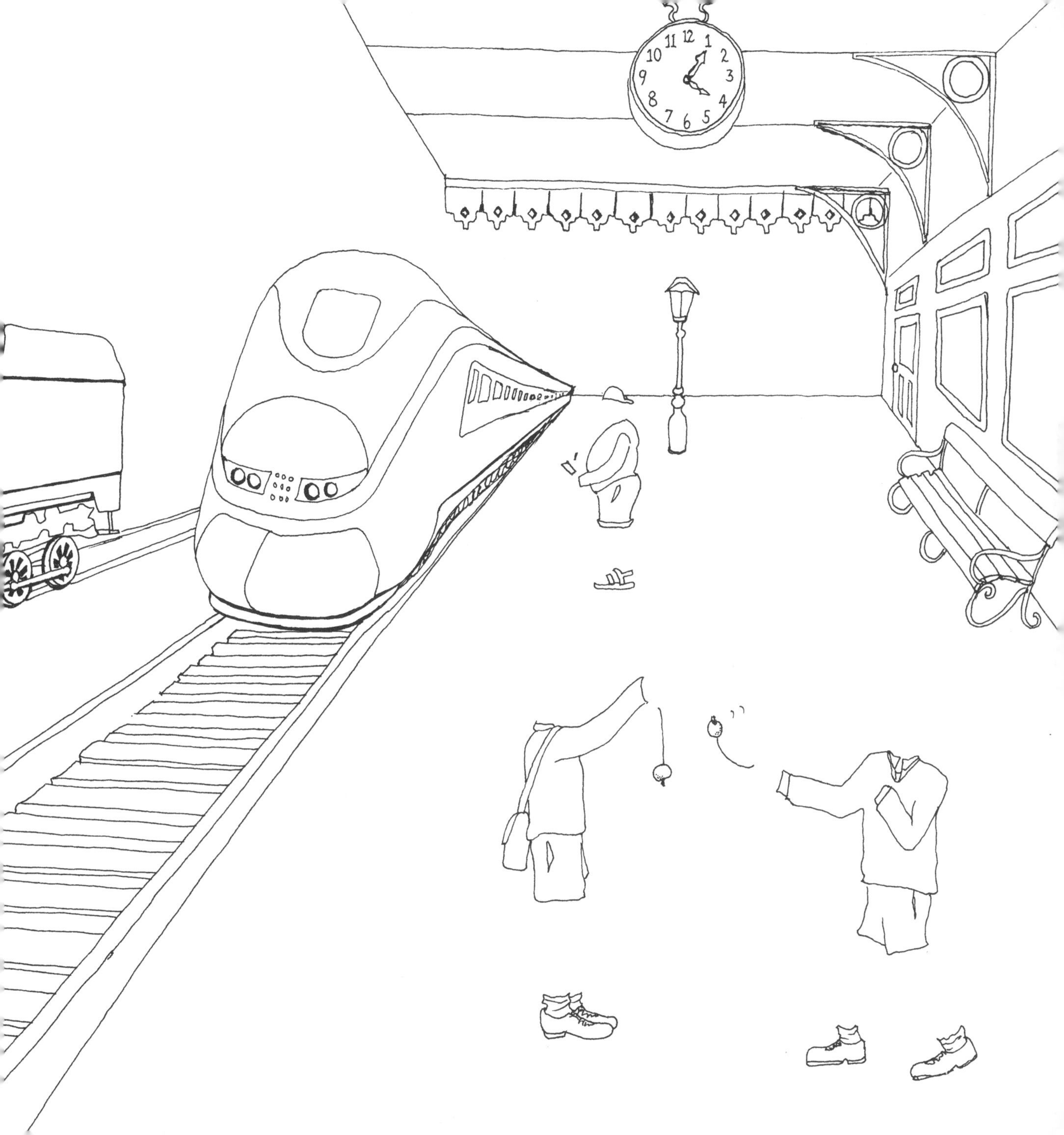

9

1

10
9
1
3
2

6
5
11
8
4

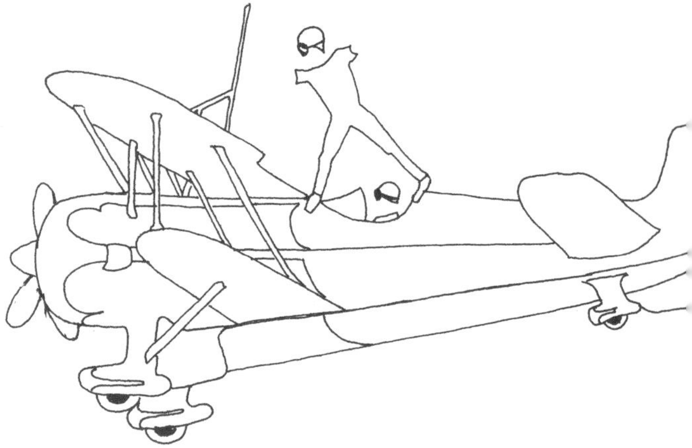

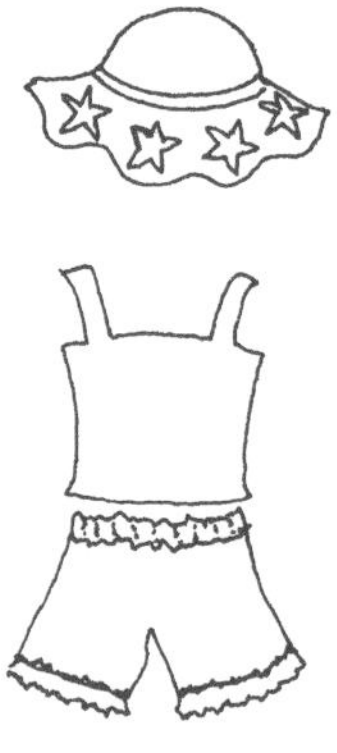

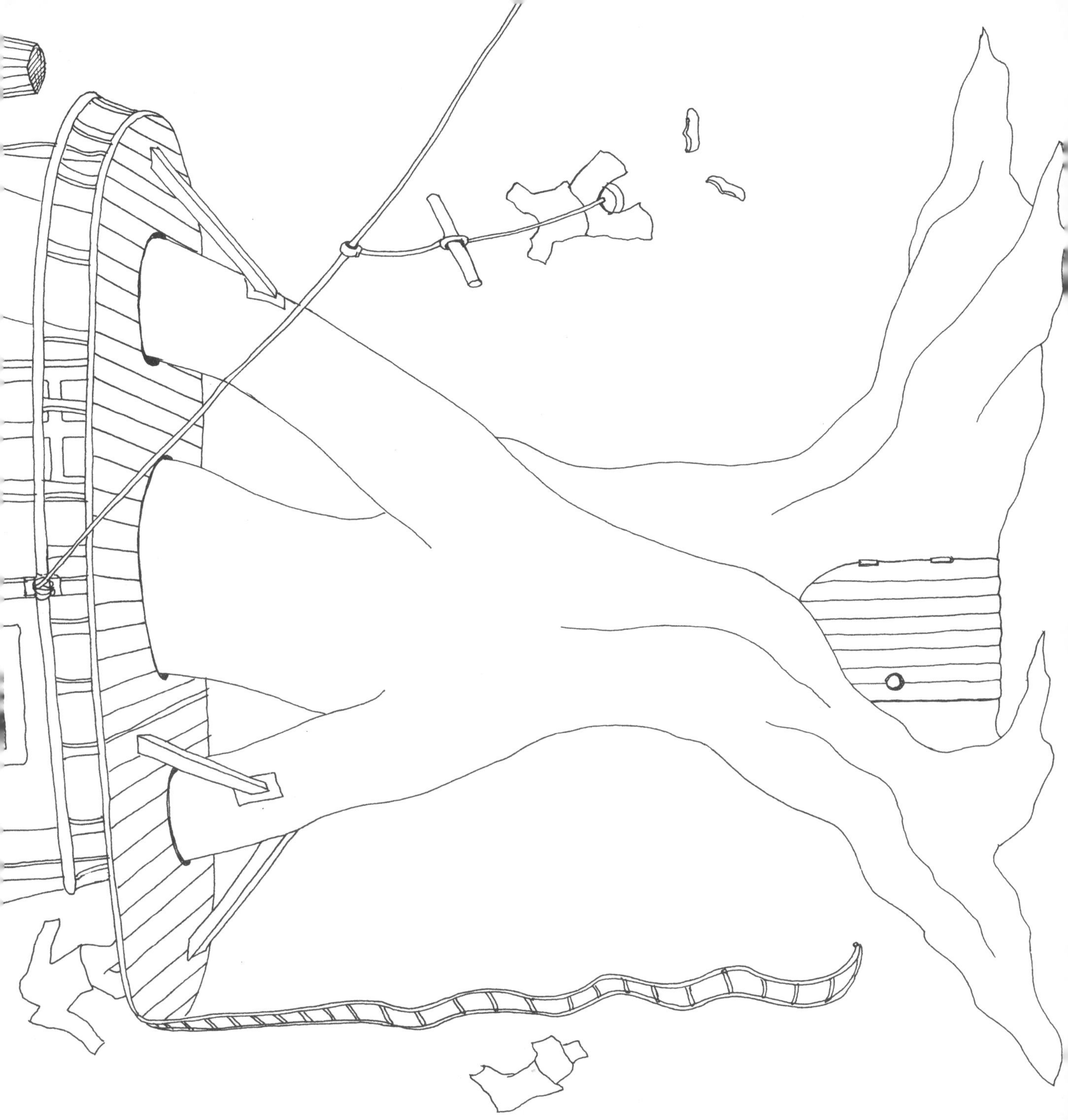

FAMILY SCALE
SALTERS

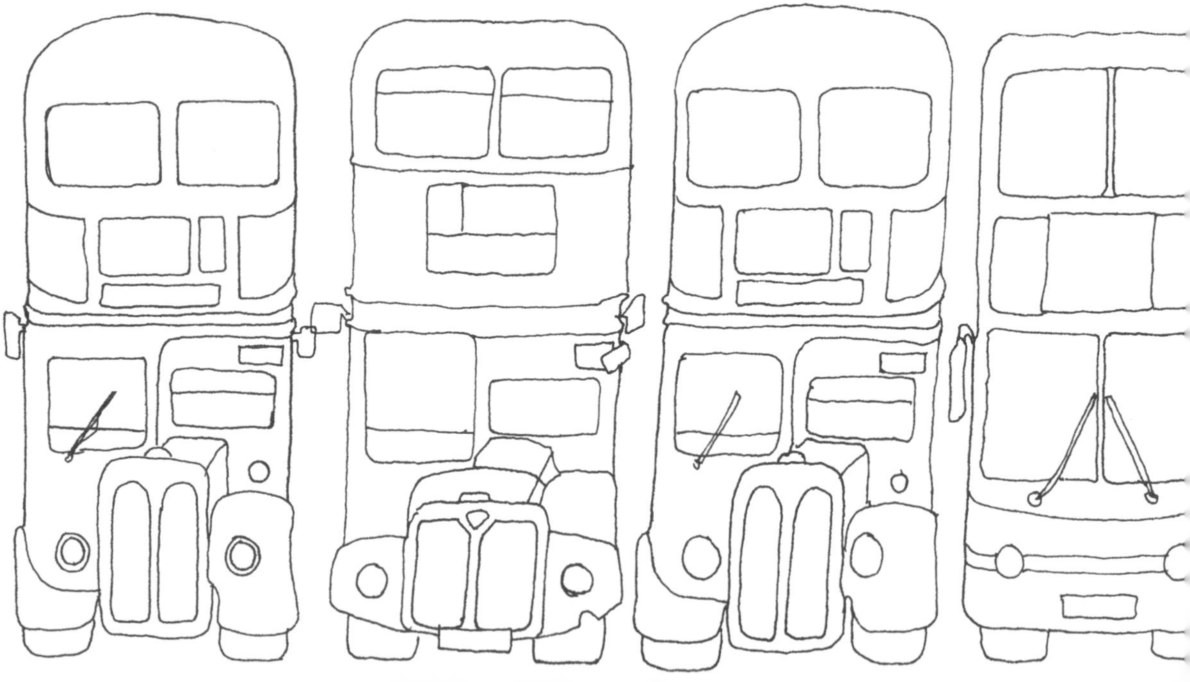

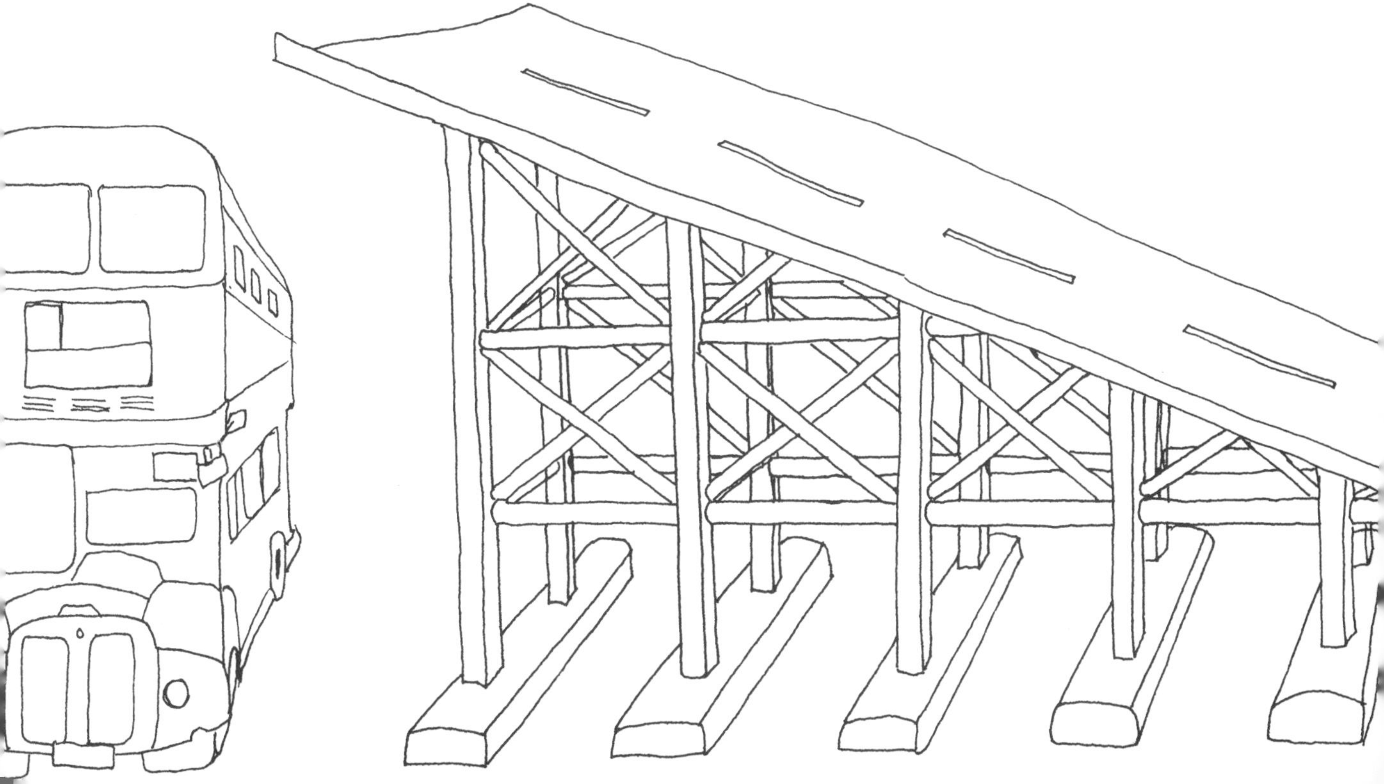

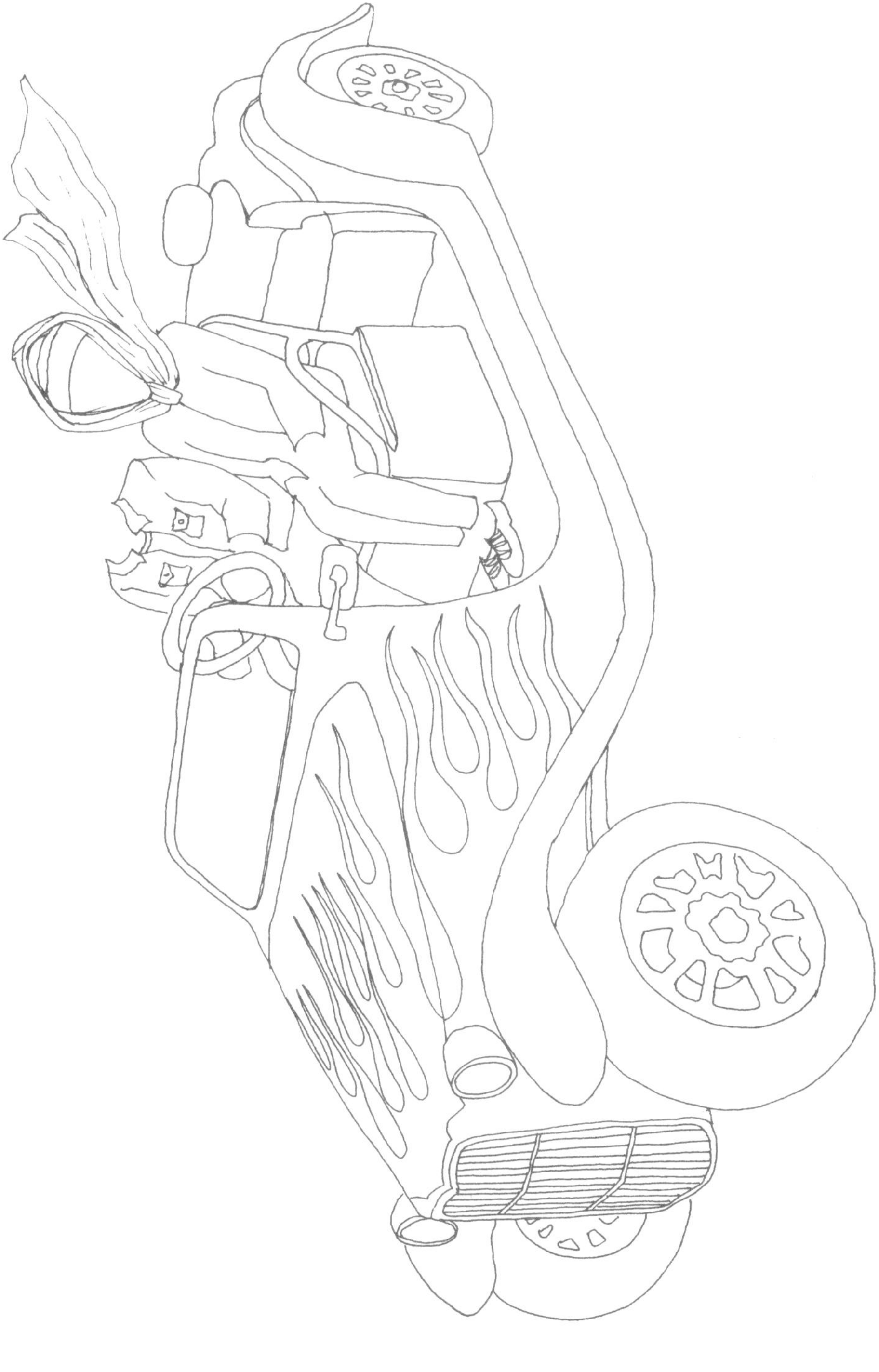

Another postcard for
you to color and mail.